evoLve

A quiet disruption for those who know something's missing.

DEBBIE PEARSON

Yesterday I was clever, so I wanted to
change the world.

Today I am wise, so I am
changing myself.

~Rumi

ISBN: 978-1-7360314-1-4
Printed in the United States of America.

This book is intended for informational and reflective purposes only.

It is not a substitute for professional medical, psychological, or legal advice.

Readers are encouraged to seek appropriate professional support for their individual circumstances.

Acknowledgment

This book would not exist without the work of Jack Russell and Glenda Otto.

Through the Self-Sustaining Leadership® model and the Essential Skills and Framworks Workbook, they gave language and structure to something I had been circling for years but could not yet name.

Their clarity around inner authority, self-trust, and leadership as an internal orientation has reshaped the way I understand growth—not as effort or improvement, but as reorientation, deeper self-awareness, and growth of capacity.

I'm deeply grateful for their thinking, their integrity, and how they make clear what so many people feel but can't quite put into words.

This book is my lived integration of that work, offered with deep respect, appreciation, and gratitude.

Contents

Introduction

This is not a how-to book. It won't give you steps. It won't tell you what to fix. And it won't help you become a better version of yourself.

If that's what you're looking for, this book will disappoint you.

You don't need more information or another framework. And you don't need to work harder on yourself.

You've already done that.

This book exists because something still hasn't integrated.

You've taken trainings, earned certifications, and done inner work.

And yet—there's a quiet restlessness you can't shake.

It's not panic.
It's not crisis.

Just a sense that something essential is missing.

That feeling isn't confusion.
It's not failure.
And it's not a sign you need more healing.

It's a signal that the way you've been orienting
yourself to growth no longer works.

Most books try to add.
This one subtracts.

It removes false causes.
False solutions.
False authority.

Not so you feel better—
but so you see more clearly.

You don't need to read this book in order.
You don't need to agree with it.
You don't even need to finish it.

Read until something shifts.
Then stop, or don't. It's your choice.

Each section stands on its own. Together, they
form a quiet disruption.

Nothing here will ask you to take action.
Nothing will invite you to change.

What happens next isn't the book's
responsibility.

Once a perception changes, behavior
reorganizes on its own.

That's what it means to evolve.

Not improvement.
Not progress.

A reorientation so complete you can't return to
how you were seeing things before.

If you feel resistance as you read, maybe don't
push past it. That resistance is information.

If something feels obvious, notice how long it's
taken to become so.

And if you find yourself thinking,
I already know this,
you may begin to notice the space between
knowing something and living it.

The book's not here to tell you what to do.

It may, however, help you see where you've
been standing in your own way.

The Lie of More

You were told that growth happens
by adding.
More insight. More tools.
More healing.

So you kept reaching for the next
thing.

And the feeling never went away.

If more were the answer …

you would already be done.

You don't feel stuck because you haven't learned enough. You feel stuck because you've been taught to look in the wrong direction.

Most heart-centered leaders believe the next course, certification, or breakthrough will finally quiet the sense that something is missing.

For a moment, it does.

Then the familiar tension returns—not louder, just steadier. More convincing.

That's not failure. That's feedback.

Evolution doesn't happen by accumulation. It happens by reorientation.

The mind is excellent at gathering. It is terrible at deciding when enough is enough.

So it keeps searching.

What you call overthinking is not confusion. It's intelligence without an anchor.

You don't need more answers.
You need a different reference point.

Evolution begins the moment you stop asking
What else do I need?
and start noticing,
What am I avoiding trusting?

Once you see that, you won't be able to unsee it.

Overthinking Is a Misuse of Power

You don't think too much.
You think instead of deciding.
Your mind isn't broken.
It's been over assigned.

Overthinking isn't confusion.
It's intelligence without direction.

Your mind was designed to solve problems.
Not to replace your authority.

When you ask it to make emotional decisions,
it panics.
So it gathers more data.
And then more.

What you call overthinking is your mind stalling
for certainty it can never provide.
The mind wants guarantees.
Life doesn't offer them.

So the mind keeps working long past
usefulness, hoping effort will eventually
produce safety.

It won't.

Clarity does not arrive through analysis.
It arrives when decision-making moves back
into alignment with your truth.

Once you stop asking your mind to do a job it
was never meant to do, it becomes a powerful
ally again.

Until then, it will keep spinning.
Not because it's failing—but because it's trying
to protect you.

Why Clarity Never Comes From the Mind

You've been waiting for clarity before
you move.
But clarity doesn't precede action.
It follows alignment.

Clarity is not a thought.

It's a state.

The mind can imagine outcomes.
It can't feel coherence.
So when you wait for mental certainty, you're
waiting for the wrong signal.

Clarity shows up as calm.
As steadiness.
As a quiet yes that doesn't argue.

The mind will always offer pros and cons.
Truth doesn't negotiate.

That's why the clearest decisions
often make the
least logical sense at first.
They don't arrive with proof.
They arrive with relief.

If you've been stuck waiting to feel "ready,"
you're not blocked.

You're listening to the wrong voice.

Clarity doesn't come from thinking.
It shows up when thinking finally steps aside.

Certifications Don't Create Conviction

You've learned enough.
You just don't trust yourself yet.

And no credential can fix that.

Conviction is not taught.

It's claimed.

Training can build skill.
It cannot build authority.

Authority comes from standing behind your own knowing—even when no one agrees.

That's why more certifications don't quiet the doubt. They only postpone the moment you choose yourself.

Conviction isn't confidence.
It's coherence.

It's what happens when your actions stop contradicting your truth.

Until then, no amount of external validation will feel like enough.

You don't need another expert to tell you what you already sense.
You need to stop outsourcing trust.

Conviction grows the moment you act without permission.

Evolution Is Not Incremental

You don't grow into alignment
slowly.
You *shift* into it.

And once you do, there's
no going back.

**Evolution isn't built step by step.
It's what reorganizes the steps.**

Incremental change works for skills.
Not for identity.

You don't become more yourself by degrees.
You become yourself by crossing a line.

That's why breakthroughs feel sudden.
They aren't new—they're released.

Evolution isn't effort.
It's orientation.

The moment fear stops deciding, everything
reorganizes around truth.

From the outside it looks like a leap.
From the inside it feels inevitable.

You don't evolve by doing more.
You evolve by seeing differently.

And once that shift happens,
you can't unknow who you are.

You Are Not Afraid of Failure

You're afraid of being exposed.
Of being misunderstood.

Of choosing yourself and
standing alone.

Fear isn't about the outcome.

It's about belonging.

Failure is clean.
It ends things.

Rejection lingers.
So you hedge.
You soften your truth.
You wait for alignment from others before
acting on your own.

Not because you lack courage.
Because belonging once felt like survival.

So you learned to read the room.
To wait.
To adjust.

But leadership was never meant to be a
group decision.

The moment you stop needing agreement,
fear loses its grip.

You don't need to be fearless.
You need to be anchored.

Why You Keep Looking Outside Yourself

You were taught that answers come from authority. Experts. Systems. Proof.

So you learned to doubt your own inner knowing.

Seeking guidance isn't the problem.

Replacing yourself is.

External input is useful—until it becomes a crutch.

Especially when the stakes feel high or when being wrong once carried consequences.

At some point, gathering more opinions isn't discernment.

It's avoidance.

Not of truth.
Of responsibility.

You already know when something fits.
You just don't trust that knowing enough to act on it.

So you ask again.
And again.

Not for clarity—but for permission.

Evolution begins when you stop asking who knows best and start asking what feels true.

Self-Trust Is a Capacity, Not a Trait

Some people don't have more
confidence.

They have more practice
standing by themselves.

**Self-trust grows through use, not
understanding.**

Self-Trust is built the same way muscles are built.
By showing up.
By bearing weight.

You don't trust yourself because you've rarely followed through on your own truth.

Each time you override it, the signal weakens.
Not because it disappears—
but because, over time, you've started to believe your voice doesn't matter.

Trust isn't restored through insight.
It's restored through action.

Small. Quiet. Unapologetic.

Every time you act in alignment, self-trust strengthens.

Every time you don't,
it waits.

Patient. Unoffended.

Peace Is Not Passive

Peace isn't what happens when
things calm down.

It's what happens when inner
conflict ends.

**Peace arrives when your truth stops
being negotiated.**

Not because the world agrees.
But because you do.

You don't feel restless because life is
demanding.

You feel restless because you're split.

One part of you knows.
Another part is afraid.

That tension costs more energy than any
schedule ever could.

Peace isn't withdrawal.
It's resolution.

When fear stops running the show, energy
returns.
Focus sharpens.
Movement feels clean.

Peace isn't the absence of action.
It's action without self-betrayal.

Love and Fear Are Operating Systems

You've treated love like a feeling and fear like a problem.

They're neither.

Love and fear don't coexist.

One runs the system.

One contracts.
One expands.
You can feel the difference
before you name it.

Fear organizes around protection.
Love organizes around truth.

Fear asks, *How do I stay safe?*
Love asks, *What is real?*

Both are efficient.
Both create results.

But only one creates coherence.

When fear is running the system, decisions
optimize for approval, certainty, and control.

When love is running the system, decisions
optimize for alignment—even when the
outcome is unknown.

You don't need to choose love as an emotion.
You choose it as an orientation.

Once you see that distinction,
you'll start recognizing which system has been
quietly in charge.

Healing Does Not Create Direction

You've healed the wounds.
Processed the past.
Made peace with the story.

And still—you're unsure where to go.

Healing removes obstacles.

It doesn't point the way.

Healing frees you from the past.
It doesn't decide the future.

Healing clears the noise.
Direction requires choice.

That's why so many people feel disoriented
after deep inner work.

They expected healing to deliver answers.

It doesn't.
It delivers capacity.

Once the pain quiets, you're left with a more
confronting question:

What do I want now that I'm not surviving?

That moment isn't a failure of healing.
It's the beginning of self-leadership.

Direction doesn't emerge from what hurt you.
It emerges from what calls you.

Inner Authority Is Not Confidence

Confidence can be borrowed.
Authority cannot.

Inner authority doesn't convince.

It stands.

Inner authority doesn't seek agreement.
It doesn't wait for reassurance.

Confidence tries to persuade.
Authority anchors.

Authority doesn't eliminate doubt.
It refuses to let doubt decide.

That's why true authority feels calm, not loud.
It doesn't need reinforcement.

Inner authority develops when you stop
outsourcing decision-making and accept the
discomfort of standing alone.

Authority doesn't rush to explain itself.
It doesn't perform for approval.
It remains steady even when misunderstood.

Not forever.
Just long enough to remember who's in
charge.

Why You Feel Split Inside

You're not conflicted because you're unclear.

You're conflicted because two truths are competing.

Inner conflict is a leadership issue, not a psychological one.

It's not confusion.
It's competing loyalties.

One part of you knows what's true.
Another part is protecting old belonging.

So you stall.
Delay.
Revisit decisions you already made.

That split drains energy.

When leadership is internalized, conflict
resolves quickly—not because fear disappears,
but because it no longer decides.

Resolution doesn't require certainty.
It requires choosing yourself.

When you stop negotiating your own knowing,
the conflict ends.

Direction Comes After Commitment

You've been waiting for fear to quiet down.

It quiets down after you choose.

The path appears after you step.

Commitment is the signal.
Clarity is the response.

Fear wants the map before movement.
Love moves and lets the map reveal itself.

That's why aligned action feels risky at first
and obvious later.

Once you commit to what's true,
clarity organizes around you.
Support appears.
Momentum builds.

Not because the world changed—
but because you stopped negotiating with
yourself.

Direction isn't found.
It's claimed.

Nothing Else Is Missing

You've been searching for the next
thing ...
as if something essential were
absent.

It isn't.

**What you've been looking for isn't
missing. It's been waiting.**

There is no final insight coming.
No moment where everything suddenly clicks
into place.

What has changed is orientation.

You can't unknow what you've seen here.

You'll notice when you're avoiding what's
already clear.

You'll feel the moment fear tries to decide for
you.

You'll recognize when you're about to
outsource your authority again.

Not because this book told you so.
But because something in you has shifted.

Evolution doesn't end here.
The need to check outside yourself does.

From this point on,
whatever comes next,
comes from you.

Thank You

Thank you for spending time with me and
with *evoLve*.
This book isn't a system.

It's a shift.

If something has reorganized for you, deeper
work may be calling—but only when you're
ready to live it, not just understand it.

I work with coaches and leaders inside a
structured, immersive system designed to
build self-sustaining inner authority, greater
self-trust, confidence, and clarity so you can
grow your business with greater ease.

I invite you to connect with me and my work:

YouTube:
@DebbiePearsonCoaching

My website:
https://www.debbiepearson.com